YES
YOU
CAN

summersdale

YES YOU CAN

An Hachette UK Company
www.hachette.co.uk

Summersdale Publishers Ltd
Part of Octopus Publishing Group Limited
Carmelite House
50 Victoria Embankment
LONDON
EC4Y 0DZ
UK

www.summersdale.com

Printed and bound in China

ISBN: 978-1-78685-979-2

Substantial discounts on bulk quantities of Summersdale books are available to corporations, professional associations and other organizations. For details contact general enquiries: telephone: +44 (0) 1243 771107 or email: enquiries@summersdale.com.

To......................................

From......................................

Keep smiling,
because life is a
beautiful thing and
there's so much to
smile about.

Marilyn Monroe

ENERGY AND PERSISTENCE CONQUER ALL THINGS.

Benjamin Franklin

If you look the right way, you can see that the whole world is a garden.

Frances Hodgson Burnett

**This life
is not for
complaint,
but for
satisfaction.**

Henry David Thoreau

The more we do, the more we can do.

William Hazlitt

The beginning is
always today.

Mary Shelley

You are never too old to set another goal or dream a new dream.

Les Brown

Expect
problems
and eat them
for breakfast.

Alfred A. Montapert

Real difficulties can be overcome; it is only the imaginary ones that are unconquerable.

Theodore N. Vail

There is nothing impossible to him who will try.

Alexander the Great

IT DOES NOT MATTER HOW SLOWLY YOU GO AS LONG AS YOU DO NOT STOP.

Confucius

If you learn
from defeat,
you haven't
really lost.

Zig Ziglar

Perseverance is failing nineteen times and succeeding the twentieth.

Julie Andrews

Be glad of life because it gives you the chance to love, to work, to play and to look up at the stars.

Henry van Dyke

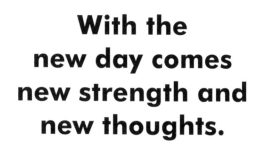

With the new day comes new strength and new thoughts.

Eleanor Roosevelt

Turn your face toward the sun and the shadows fall behind you.

Māori proverb

MISTAKES ARE THE PORTALS OF DISCOVERY.

James Joyce

I don't measure a man's success by how high he climbs but how high he bounces when he hits bottom.

George S. Patton

It's never too
late – never too
late to start over,
never too late
to be happy.

Jane Fonda

THE ROUGHEST ROADS OFTEN LEAD TO THE TOP.

Christina Aguilera

May you live every day of your life.

Jonathan Swift

I can,
therefore
I am.

Simone Weil

The man who
removes a mountain
begins by carrying
away small stones.

Chinese proverb

IF
OPPORTUNITY
DOESN'T
KNOCK,
BUILD
A DOOR.

Milton Berle

I'd rather regret the things I've done than regret the things I haven't done.

Lucille Ball

There are no
traffic jams
along the
extra mile.

Roger Staubach

**We are all in
the gutter, but
some of us
are looking
at the stars.**

Oscar Wilde

Only those who will risk going too far can possibly find out how far one can go.

T. S. Eliot

**Act as if what
you do makes
a difference.
It does.**

William James

When everything seems to be going against you, remember the airplane takes off against the wind, not with it.

Henry Ford

What you do today
can improve all
your tomorrows.

Ralph Marston

It's hard to beat
a person who
never gives up.

Babe Ruth

Do your thing
and don't care
if they like it.

Tina Fey

IF IT DOESN'T CHALLENGE YOU, IT DOESN'T CHANGE YOU.

Fred DeVito

Your present circumstances don't determine where you can go; they merely determine where you start.

Nido Qubein

Victory belongs to the most persevering.

Napoleon Bonaparte

Turn your wounds into wisdom.

Oprah Winfrey

Anyone can hide.
Facing up to
things, working
through them,
that's what makes
you strong.

Sarah Dessen

When you know yourself, you are empowered. When you accept yourself, you are invincible.

Tina Lifford

You are the
hero of your
own story.

Joseph Campbell

Just don't give up trying to do what you really want to do.

Ella Fitzgerald

Never give up then, for that is just the place and time that the tide will turn.

Harriet Beecher Stowe

ONE MAY
WALK OVER
THE HIGHEST
MOUNTAIN
ONE STEP AT
A TIME.

John Wanamaker

I am learning
every day to allow
the space between
where I am and
where I want to be
to inspire me and
not terrify me.

Tracee Ellis Ross

Success
always
demands
a greater
effort.

Winston Churchill

One can
never consent
to creep when
one feels an
impulse to soar.

Helen Keller

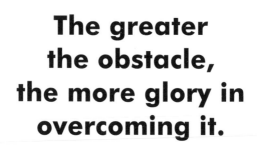

The greater the obstacle, the more glory in overcoming it.

Molière

Some days there won't be a song in your heart. Sing anyway.

Emory Austin

SPEAK UP. BELIEVE IN YOURSELF. TAKE RISKS.

Sheryl Sandberg

Love yourself for who you are and just keep going.

Demi Lovato

If we are
facing in the
right direction,
all we have
to do is keep
on walking.

Buddhist proverb

YOU ARE BRAVER THAN YOU BELIEVE.

A. A. Milne

Fall seven times, stand up eight.

Japanese proverb

Stones in the road? I save every single one, and one day I'll build a castle.

Fernando Pessoa

Nothing can dim the
light which shines
from within.

Maya Angelou

IF YOU HAVE THE COURAGE TO BEGIN, YOU HAVE THE COURAGE TO SUCCEED.

David Viscott

Let me tell you the secret that has led to my goal. My strength lies solely in my tenacity.

Louis Pasteur

Ever tried.
Ever failed.
No matter.
Try again.
Fail again.
Fail better.

Samuel Beckett

Your victory is right around the corner. Never give up.

Nicki Minaj

**Every day,
in every way,
I'm getting better
and better.**

Émile Coué

**You have to
be unique,
and different,
and shine in
your own way.**

Lady Gaga

I am no bird;
and no net
ensnares me:
I am a free human
being with an
independent will.

Charlotte Brontë

Sometimes the
smallest step in
the right direction
ends up being the
biggest step of
your life.

Naeem Callaway

The future rewards those who press on. I don't have time to feel sorry for myself. I don't have time to complain. I'm going to press on.

Barack Obama

Always be a first-rate version of yourself, instead of a second-rate version of somebody else.

Judy Garland

IF YOU OBEY ALL THE RULES, YOU MISS ALL THE FUN.

Katharine Hepburn

Always do what you are afraid to do.

Ralph Waldo Emerson

Change your thoughts and you change your world.

Norman Vincent Peale

It is often in the darkest skies that we see the brightest stars.

Richard Paul Evans

Be **bold** or *italic*.
Never just regular.

Anonymous

When you're true to who you are, amazing things happen.

Deborah Norville

The past
cannot be
changed.
The future
is yet in
your power.

Mary Pickford

The greatest danger in life is not to take the adventure.

George Mallory

Be strong,
be fearless,
be beautiful.

Misty Copeland

YOU MISS 100 PER CENT OF THE SHOTS YOU DON'T TAKE.

Wayne Gretzky

I always believe
that the sky is
the beginning
of the limit.

MC Hammer

Doubt whom you will, but never yourself.

Christian Nestell Bovee

I couldn't find the sports car of my dreams, so I built it myself.

Ferdinand Porsche

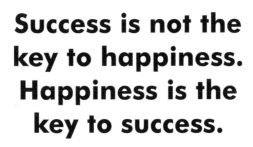

Success is not the key to happiness. Happiness is the key to success.

Anonymous

A wise man will make more opportunities than he finds.

Francis Bacon

YOUR LIFE IS A BOOK; MAKE IT A BESTSELLER.

Shanon Grey

The sweetest pleasures are those which are hardest to be won.

Giacomo Casanova

Don't be afraid
to give up the
good to go for
the great.

John D. Rockefeller

DON'T WAIT TO BE SURE. MOVE, MOVE, MOVE.

Miranda July

The great end of life is not knowledge but action.

Thomas Henry Huxley

I don't focus on what I'm up against. I focus on my goals and I try to ignore the rest.

Venus Williams

Live as if
you were to die
tomorrow. Learn
as if you were to
live forever.

Mahatma Gandhi

THE BEST WAY TO PREDICT THE FUTURE IS TO INVENT IT.

Alan Kay

Aim for the moon. If you miss, you may hit a star.

W. Clement Stone

Success is often achieved by those who don't know that failure is inevitable.

Coco Chanel

Nothing is impossible. The word itself says "I'm possible"!

Audrey Hepburn

Do a little more each day than you think you possibly can.

Lowell Thomas

Ordinary me can achieve something extraordinary by giving that little bit extra.

Bear Grylls

We must have perseverance and, above all, confidence in ourselves.

Marie Curie

Follow your
passions, follow
your heart, and
the things you
need will come.

Elizabeth Taylor

Keep trying until
you have no more
chances left.

Aimee Carter

If my mind
can conceive it,
and my heart
can believe it,
I know I can
achieve it.

Jesse Jackson

THE MOST EFFECTIVE WAY TO DO IT, IS TO DO IT.

Amelia Earhart

Always go with your passions. Never ask yourself if it's realistic or not.

Deepak Chopra

The strongest steel is forged in the hottest fire.

Proverb

Champions keep playing until they get it right.

Billie Jean King

When life throws
tomatoes at you,
make Bloody Marys!

Anonymous

Change your life today. Don't gamble on the future, act now, without delay.

Simone de Beauvoir

I couldn't wait for success, so I went ahead without it.

Jonathan Winters

The best way to
not feel hopeless
is to get up and
do something.
Don't wait for
good things to
happen to you.

Barack Obama

You cannot swim for new horizons until you have courage to lose sight of the shore.

William Faulkner

DON'T COUNT THE DAYS; MAKE THE DAYS COUNT.

Muhammad Ali

If things
don't work out
the way you want,
hold your head up
high and be proud.
And try again.

Sarah Dessen

Courage is the ladder on which all the other virtues mount.

Clare Boothe Luce

It will never
rain roses:
when we want to
have more roses
we must plant
more trees.

George Eliot

It takes just one star to pierce a universe of darkness. Never give up.

Richelle E. Goodrich

You're the blacksmith of your own happiness.

Swedish proverb

YOU HAVE TO BELIEVE IN YOURSELF AND BE STRONG.

Adriana Lima

The human capacity for burden is like bamboo – far more flexible than you'd ever believe at first glance.

Jodi Picoult

Keep the faith,
don't lose your
perseverance and
always trust your
gut instinct.

Paula Abdul

THERE ARE NO SHORTCUTS TO ANY PLACE WORTH GOING.

Beverly Sills

Don't be discouraged. It's often the last key in the bunch that opens the lock.

Anonymous

The difference between a successful person and others is not a lack of strength... but rather a lack of will.

Vince Lombardi

Believe you
can and you're
halfway there.

Theodore Roosevelt

SET YOUR GOALS HIGH AND DON'T STOP UNTIL YOU GET THERE.

Bo Jackson

It isn't where you came from; it's where you're going that counts.

Ella Fitzgerald

The greatest oak was once a little nut that held its ground.

Anonymous

Through perseverance many people win success out of what seemed destined to be certain failure.

Benjamin Disraeli

Just because you fail once, it doesn't mean you're going to fail at everything.

Marilyn Monroe

If you're presenting yourself with confidence, you can pull off pretty much anything.

Katy Perry

In case of doubt,
push on just
a little further
and then keep
on pushing.

George S. Patton

Giving up is
the only sure
way to fail.

Gena Showalter

Find out who you are and be that person... Find that truth, live that truth and everything else will come.

Ellen DeGeneres

Success is
no accident.
It is hard work,
perseverance,
learning, studying,
sacrifice and most
of all, love of what
you are doing.

Pelé

IT'S ALWAYS TOO SOON TO QUIT.

Norman Vincent Peale

The scariest moment is always just before you start.

Stephen King

You have to believe in yourself when no one else does – that makes you a winner right there.

Venus Williams

As soon as you trust yourself, you will know how to live.

Johann Wolfgang von Goethe

Pride is holding
your head up when
everyone around you
has theirs bowed.
Courage is what
makes you do it.

Bryce Courtenay

BE YOURSELF ALWAYS, EXPRESS YOURSELF AND HAVE FAITH IN YOURSELF.

Bruce Lee

Whether you think you can or you think you can't, you're right.

Henry Ford

It is never too late
to be what you
might have been.

Adelaide Anne Procter

When the world says, "Give up", hope whispers, "Try it one more time".

Anonymous

SAIL AWAY
FROM THE
SAFE
HARBOUR...
EXPLORE.
DREAM.
DISCOVER.

H. Jackson Brown Jr

The biggest
adventure you can
ever take is to
live the life of
your dreams.

Oprah Winfrey

When I started
counting my
blessings,
my whole
life turned
around.

Willie Nelson

You can have
anything you
want if you are
willing to give up
the belief that
you can't have it.

Robert Anthony

The potential for greatness lives within each of us.

Wilma Rudolph

To love
oneself is the
beginning
of a lifelong
romance.

Oscar Wilde

IT IS NOT THE MOUNTAIN WE CONQUER, BUT OURSELVES.

Edmund Hillary

No one succeeds without effort... Those who succeed owe their success to perseverance.

Ramana Maharshi

If your heart is
broken, make art
with the pieces.

Shane Koyczan

DO NOT WAIT; THE TIME WILL NEVER BE "JUST RIGHT".

Napoleon Hill

It is your reaction to adversity, not adversity itself, that determines how your life's story will develop.

Dieter F. Uchtdorf

I can be changed by what happens to me. But I refuse to be reduced by it.

Maya Angelou

The question isn't
who is going to
let me; it's who is
going to stop me.

Ayn Rand

EVERYTHING YOU'VE EVER WANTED IS ON THE OTHER SIDE OF FEAR.

George Addair

No matter how much falls on us, we keep plowing ahead. That's the only way to keep the roads clear.

Greg Kincaid

Dream lofty dreams, and as you dream, so shall you become.

James Allen

Everything you can imagine is real.

Pablo Picasso

The envious moment is flying now, now, while we're speaking: seize the day.

Horace

If you're interested in finding out more about our books, find us on Facebook at Summersdale Publishers and follow us on Twitter at @Summersdale.

www.summersdale.com